Preface

Welcome to a journey of empowerment, self-discovery, and transformation. This book is a beacon of hope for anyone affected by diabetes, offering a comprehensive guide to not just managing this condition but thriving in spite of it. It's about making choices that lead to a healthier, happier, and more fulfilling life.

Triumph in the Face of Adversaries
Diabetes is a formidable adversary, but it is not unbeatable. In these pages, we will explore the power of lifestyle changes, sound choices, and informed decisions. And together, we will break down the barriers that often stand in the way of effective diabetes management.

In the seven chapters that follow, we look deep into the obstacles of living with diabetes:

1. We'll discuss adherence to lifestyle recommendations, self-compliance, and the art of saying "no" when needed.
2. You'll learn to navigate medical advice with confidence, question the status quo when it comes to treatment, and work collaboratively with healthcare professionals.

Exercise, a cornerstone of diabetes management, is unleashed with insights into building muscle and optimizing glycogen storage. We will not only swim into how easy it can be to to incorporate exercise into our routine, but also dive head first into the latest research on diabetes, separating fact from fiction and offering a glimpse into the future of diabetes care.

Lastly, we'll explore dietary approaches gaining recognition for their potential to regulate blood glucose (aka blood sugar) levels effectively.

Throughout this book, you'll find a balance of scientific knowledge, practical tips, and realistic methods to turning your condition around for lasting change. Whether you are newly diagnosed or have been living with diabetes for years, these pages are designed to inspire, educate, and empower you.

Copyright

First Edition, 2020; Second Edition, 2023
ISBN:9781943117024 (Print Edition)

Copyright © 2020 by:
Dr. Jasmine Blake Hollywood

All rights reserved.

No part of this book may be reproduced in any form; or by any electronic, mechanical or any other means including information storage and retrieval systems without expressed permission in writing from the publisher or Jasmine Blake Hollywood, except by reviewers who may quote passages in their review.

Editing by:
EatitUP™ Editing Team

Authored by:
Dr. Jasmine Blake Hollywood
DCN, LDN, CNS, BA-Psy, CRPS, ORDM

Printed, written, and bound in United States

Published by:
Discover Your Greatest Self™

True Paleo Inc.
PO Box 130282
Tampa, FL. 33681
www.jasmineblake.com

Table of Contents

Introduction — 1

Chapter 1: Adherence to Lifestyle Recommendations — 3
- Understanding the Importance of Adherence — 4
- Overcoming Common Barriers to Adherence — 5
- Setting Realistic Goals for Sustainable Change — 7

Chapter 2: Self-Compliance and Avoiding Excuses — 11
- The Psychology of Self-Compliance — 12
- Recognizing and Overcoming Excuses — 14
- Building a Supportive Network for Accountability — 16

Chapter 3: Saying No and Prioritizing Self-Care — 19
- Putting Yourself First: Why It Matters — 20
- Strategies for Saying No Without Guilt — 22
- Balancing Responsibilities and Self-Care — 24

Chapter 4: Navigating Medical Advice — 27
- Common Misconceptions About Diabetes Treatment — 28
- Questioning Doctors' Recommendations: When and How — 29
- Collaborating with Healthcare Professionals for Optimal Care — 32

Chapter 5: Research and Understanding Diabetes — 35
- Unpacking the Types and Causes of Diabetes — 36
- Recent Advancements in Diabetes Research — 39
- The Future of Diabetes Treatment and Prevention — 41

Chapter 6: Exercise and Blood Glucose Regulation — 43
- The Role of Exercise in Diabetes Management — 44
- Building Muscle to Improve Glycogen Storage — 46
- Creating an Effective Exercise Routine — 48

Chapter 7: The Paleo Diet for Blood Glucose Regulation — 51
- Exploring the Paleo Diet and Its Principles — 52
- The Impact of Paleo on Blood Glucose Levels — 54
- Practical Tips for Incorporating Paleo into Your Lifestyle — 56

Introduction

Introduction

In a world filled with constant motion and ever-evolving lifestyles, one constant remains: the importance of health. And at the heart of many health journeys lies a condition that affects more than 130 million in the United States, diabetes. Whether you are suffering from diabetes yourself, supporting a loved one on their journey, or simply seeking to understand this complex condition better, this book is your guide to empowerment and transformation.

Diabetes is more than a diagnosis; it's a daily companion, a puzzle to solve, and a call to action. It challenges us to make choices, sometimes tough ones, about our lives, our habits, and our well-being. But here's the good news: you have the power to shape the course of your health journey. You have the ability to turn challenges into opportunities, and hurdles into stepping stones toward better health.

This book is not just another medical manual; it's an alternative roadmap to a life well-lived with diabetes. It's about understanding the importance of adherence to lifestyle recommendations, not just as a set of rules to follow, but as a pathway to freedom and better health. It's about embracing self-compliance and learning to navigate a world filled with excuses and temptations.

We'll explore the art of saying "no" when needed and prioritizing self-care without guilt. We'll take a deeper look into the confusing world of medical advice, questioning recommendations when they don't align with your goals, and creating a collaborative relationship with the right practitioner.

Exercise, often seen as a chore, becomes a source of empowerment as we uncover its role in muscle development and glycogen storage to maintain this lingering condition. We'll journey through the latest research on diabetes, separating myths from facts and glimpsing into the exciting future of diabetes care.

Lastly, we'll explore the latest dietary approach gaining recognition for its potential to regulate blood glucose levels effectively. You'll find practical tips, methods that work, and a wealth of knowledge to equip you with the tools you need for your health journey.

This book is your invitation to take control, to become the author of your diabetes story.

Adherence to Lifestyle Recommendations

Understanding the Importance of Adherence

Unlike normal guides for individuals with diabetes that lecture on general diabetes overviews, medications and insulin, complications and reduction, blood sugar management, practical tips, medical guidance, and dietary guidance, this guide will focus on what most educators are reluctant to discuss, adherence, self-compliance, prioritizing self-care, learning to say no, navigating medical advice, research and understanding diabetes, why exercise is important, and how exactly to eat for this condition. However, first we will start with adherence because this is the most important part of why many people begin to have blood glucose dysregulation in the first place.

When it comes to managing diabetes, adherence is not merely a buzzword but a cornerstone of effective self-care. It's the commitment you make to yourself, a pact that transcends numbers on a glucose monitor and transcends into a profound understanding of what it means to live well with diabetes. Imagine adherence as the compass guiding you through the maze of diabetes management. At its core, it encompasses following your primary care provider's recommendations, including medication regimens, dietary guidelines, and exercise routines. But it's more than a checklist; it's a mindset.

The Domino Effect of Adherence

Consider adherence as the initial push of a domino in a carefully constructed chain. When that first piece falls in place, it triggers a cascading series of positive outcomes. Adherence to your medication regimen, for instance, helps regulate blood glucose levels. This, in turn, reduces the risk of diabetes-related complications such as cardiovascular disease, kidney disease, vision problems, and nerve damage. However, adherence to medication is not the only topic that needs to be addressed.

Adhering to dietary recommendations cultivates a healthier relationship with food. It empowers you to make informed choices about what you consume, stabilizing blood glucose levels and promoting overall well-being. As you witness these improvements, your motivation to adhere grows stronger, creating a self-sustaining cycle of wellness. Hence, adhering to dietary changes is essential for the maintenance and reduction of diabetes.

The Role of Consistency

Consistency is the heartbeat of adherence. It's not about perfection; rather, it's the steady rhythm of making daily choices that align with your health goals. For example, consistency bridges the gap between intention and action. Imagine a scenario where you diligently follow your prescribed medication for a few days, then you begin to skip doses out of convenience or forgetfulness. This inconsistency can lead to erratic blood glucose levels, making it challenging to manage your condition effectively. This same concept also applies to diet and exercise. The more a person skips these daily "must-do's", the worse blood glucose levels become. Therefore, maintaining a consistent dietary and exercise routine can significantly enhance your ability to keep diabetes in check.

Adherence as Empowerment
Adherence is not a restrictive concept that stifles your freedom; it's a pathway to empowerment. When you consistently follow your diabetes management plan, you regain control over your life, improving your health. You become an active participant in your well-being journey rather than a passive observer of your condition. As you witness the positive effects of your choices, you gain confidence in your ability to tackle the challenges diabetes presents. This newfound resilience can transform your perception of diabetes from a burden to an opportunity for personal growth.

Overcoming Common Barriers to Adherence
The path to successful diabetes management is paved with good intentions, but it is often dotted with obstacles. It's crucial to recognize that adherence is not a straightforward journey; it's a road that can be marred by common barriers. These barriers are the sharks that stand in the way of your quest for optimal health, but with the right strategies and mindset, they can be conquered.

Barrier 1: Fear and Denial
One of the most significant barriers to adherence is fear, often accompanied by denial. The diagnosis of diabetes can be overwhelming, and it's natural to want to deny its existence or downplay its severity. This fear and denial can manifest as avoidance of primary care physician and licensed dietitian-nutritionist appointments, reluctance to check blood glucose levels, or even neglecting prescribed recommendations. Therefore, facing your fears is the first step toward overcoming them. Educate yourself about your condition, its implications, and the benefits of proper management. Seek support to address your concerns.

Barrier 2: Lifestyle and Habits
Adhering to a new lifestyle and breaking old habits can be challenging. It

may involve significant changes in dietary choices, exercise routines, and daily routines. The comfort of familiar habits can make it tempting to revert to old ways, even if they are detrimental to your health. Hence, it's best to start small and gradually introduce changes into your daily life. Set realistic goals that align with your long-term health objectives. Seek support from friends and family who can join you on your journey or provide encouragement. Remember that habits take time to form, and setbacks are a natural part of the process. Be patient with yourself.

Barrier 3: Social and Peer Pressure
Social gatherings, family events, and peer pressure can pose significant challenges to adherence. These situations may tempt you to deviate from your diabetes management plan to fit in or avoid awkward conversations. Thus, open communication is key. Inform your close friends and family about your health goals and the importance of adherence. Engage in discussions about how they can support you during social events. In many cases, loved ones will be willing to make accommodations or provide encouragement once they understand your perspective. Additionally, seek out social support groups or online communities where you can connect with others facing similar challenges.

Barrier 4: Emotional Well-being
Emotional well-being plays a vital role in adherence. Stress, anxiety, depression, and other emotional factors can disrupt your adherence efforts. Emotional eating, for instance, is a common coping mechanism that can lead to unhealthy food choices. One way to overcome this is to prioritize your mental health by seeking support from mental health professionals. Also, engage in stress-reduction techniques such as mindfulness, meditation, expressive art, or yoga. Recognize that addressing emotional well-being is an integral part of diabetes management, and seeking help is a sign of strength.

Barrier 5: Financial Constraints
The cost of diabetes management, including dietary appointments, medications, testing supplies, and healthier food options, can be a significant barrier. Financial constraints may lead to compromises in adherence. Therefore, exploring resources available to assist with the cost of diabetes management, such as government programs, insurance coverage, or patient funded assistance programs offered by companies can help ease these limitations. Additionally, consult with your practitioner to discuss cost-effective treatment options and strategies for

managing expenses can help open doorways and reduce additional costs.

Barrier 6: Lack of Education
One of the most significant barriers is misinformation. Lack of understanding diabetes and its management can hinder adherence. Without proper knowledge, individuals may struggle to make informed decisions. One way to overcome this is to invest time in learning about diabetes and its management. Reliable sources of information, such as reputable websites that utilize referred research and not basic blogs, and educational materials, can empower you with the knowledge needed to make informed choices.

Setting Realistic Goals for Sustainable Change
In the world of diabetes, the journey toward better health begins with a single step, setting realistic goals. Goals are not just milestones; they are the guiding stars that lead you through the maze of lifestyle changes. They provide direction, motivation, and a sense of purpose. However, not all goals are created equal. To make progress that lasts, it's essential to craft goals that are both achievable and sustainable.

Understanding the Power of Goals
Goals serve as the foundation upon which your actions are built. They give you a clear sense of purpose, transforming vague intentions into concrete plans. Consider a scenario where your goal is to achieve better blood glucose control. This overarching goal can be broken down into smaller, actionable steps, such as drinking one less soda per day, eating one salad daily, opting out of take-out and making lunch to bring to work 3 days per week, or engaging in regular physical activity. These individual steps can become your roadmap, guiding you toward your ultimate destination.

The Pitfall of Unrealistic Expectations
Setting goals is an art, and like any art form, it requires finesse. One common mistake is the establishment of overly ambitious goals, such as never dining out again, avoiding festivities because of the foods that accompany these types of places, or completely eliminate all sugar from your diet overnight. Setting a goals like this may prove unattainable and unsustainable. While aiming high can be motivating, it's crucial to ensure that your goals are within reach. Unrealistic expectations can lead to frustration, burnout, and ultimately, abandonment of your health objectives. These drastic changes can lead to feelings of failure, that the system of goal making does not work, or even deprivation and cravings, making it more likely that you'll eventually revert to old habits.

The SMART Approach
A practical framework for setting realistic goals is the SMART criteria:

Specific
Clearly define your goal. Instead of a vague aim like "improve my diet," specify "reduce sugary snacks in my diet to once a week."

Measurable
Establish criteria to measure your progress. Use quantifiable metrics, such as "reduce my A1c by 0.5% in three months."

Achievable
Ensure that your goal is attainable given your current circumstances. It should challenge you but remain within the realm of possibility.

Relevant
Align your goal with your long-term health objectives. It should be relevant to your unique needs and circumstances.

Time-Bound
Set a clear timeframe for achieving your goal. For example, "achieve my goal of walking 30 minutes every day within the next two months."

Breaking Down Complex Goals
Complex goals can be intimidating, but they become more manageable when broken down into smaller, achievable steps. Consider the example of improving your diet. Instead of attempting a complete dietary overhaul, start by focusing on one aspect, such as reducing sugary snacks. Once you've successfully integrated this change into your routine, move on to the next goal, like increasing your daily vegetable intake. This incremental approach not only makes the journey more manageable but also increases your chances of long-term success.

The Role of Flexibility
While setting specific and measurable goals is essential, it's equally vital to embrace flexibility. Life is dynamic, and unexpected challenges may arise. Acknowledge that occasional setbacks are part of the process. Instead of viewing them as failures, see them as opportunities to learn and adjust your goals as needed. For instance, if you miss a few days of exercise due to a busy schedule or illness, it doesn't mean you should abandon your fitness goal altogether. Adjust your timeline and strive for consistency in the coming

weeks. Remember that setbacks are not roadblocks; they are detours on the path to sustainable change.

The Power of Support
Setting and achieving goals is not a solitary endeavor. It's immensely beneficial to share your goals with a supportive network of friends, family, or healthcare professionals. Their encouragement, accountability, and guidance can significantly enhance your chances of success.

Consider involving a licensed dietitian-nutritionist in your goal-setting process. They can provide expert guidance, tailor goals to your specific needs, and monitor your progress. Additionally, sharing your goals with loved ones or professionals that care can create an environment of support and motivation.

Celebrating Milestones
In the pursuit of long-term change, it's essential to celebrate milestones along the way. Recognize and reward yourself for your achievements, no matter how small they may seem. These celebrations serve as positive reinforcement, reinforcing your commitment to your goals.

For instance, if you've successfully maintained a daily walking routine for a month, treat yourself to a leisurely nature hike or a favorite healthy snack. Notice, the term "favorite healthy snack", as many people confuse this with favorite or preferred food. When celebrating a milestone. It is important to understand that rewards should involve doing things for yourself that still fall within your health care plan and routine. These rewards not only mark your progress but also contribute to the positive associations you build with your goals.

The Journey Toward Sustainable Change
Setting realistic goals is not a one-time event; it's an ongoing process. You will continue to make goals as your progress. As you achieve your initial objectives, new ones will emerge, reflecting your evolving health aspirations. After some time, these new goal become easier to make, easier to manage, and easier accomplish. Remember that the journey toward sustainable change is a marathon, not a sprint. It's about building a foundation of healthier habits that stand the test of time.

End of Chapter Exercise:
Write down three small SMART goals to start with.

Adherence to Lifestyle Recommendations

Goal 1:

_____

_____

_____

Goal 2:

_____

_____

_____

Goal 3:

_____

_____

_____

Date or time frame to achieve:

Goal 1:

_____

Goal 2:

_____

Goal 3:

_____

Self-Compliance and Avoiding Excuses

The Psychology of Self-Compliance

When it comes to management of diabetes, adherence to prescribed treatments and lifestyle changes is more than a matter of following a set of instructions. It's a complex combination of thoughts, emotions, and behaviors. Understanding the psychology of self-compliance is key to unraveling human behavior and improving the way we engage with our health.

The Cognitive Aspects

The decision to adhere to a diabetes management plan often begins with cognitive processes. It's the rational part of our mind that assesses the potential risks and benefits of adherence. For individuals with diabetes, this may involve weighing the consequences of skipping a meal, the impact of dietary choices and food purchase options, or opting out of exercise knowing the benefits of engaging in regular fitness.

Cognitive Biases

Cognitive processes are not always purely logical. Cognitive biases, such as optimism bias (believing that negative events are less likely to happen to us) or present bias (prioritizing immediate rewards over long-term benefits), can influence our decision-making. For example, someone might underestimate the long-term risks of uncontrolled blood glucose because they focus on short-term comfort by eating poor choices of food.

Information Processing

Effective self-compliance often hinges on the quality of information processing. This includes understanding and interpreting medical advice accurately. Misinterpretations or misunderstandings can lead to non-compliance. Clear communication with your practitioners and seeking clarification when in doubt is essential.

The Emotional Component

Emotions are powerful drivers of behavior. Emotions can either motivate or hinder self-compliance. Fear, anxiety, and guilt may arise from the fear of complications or the stress of managing a chronic condition. On the other hand, positive emotions like hope and determination can fuel adherence.

Fear and Anxiety

Fear of the unknown or the anticipation of pain and discomfort can lead to avoidance behaviors. For instance, someone might avoid checking their blood glucose because they fear the results or the pain of pricking their finger. Acknowledging and addressing these fears is vital for improving self-compliance.

Guilt and Shame
Individuals with diabetes sometimes experience guilt or shame related to their condition. They may blame themselves for their diagnosis or feel ashamed of perceived failures in managing their health. These emotions can be detrimental to self-compliance and mental well-being.

Behavioral Patterns
Self-compliance is ultimately expressed through behavior. It's about translating intentions into actions. This is where habits, routines, and reinforcement play a crucial role.

Habit Formation
Habits are powerful in driving behavior. Creating healthy habits, such as eating or exercising at the same time every day, can simplify self-compliance. Habits rely less on conscious decision-making and more on automatic responses. This is why incorporating them is essential.

Self-Efficacy
Self-efficacy, or one's belief in their ability to achieve a specific goal, plays a significant role in self-compliance. Those with high self-efficacy are more likely to persist in the face of challenges. Building self-efficacy involves setting achievable goals, gaining experience, and celebrating successes, no matter how small. Thus, believing in sour ability to achieve something sets the stage for our progress.

The Role of Motivation
Motivation is the engine that propels self-compliance. It's the inner drive to adhere to a diabetes management plan. Understanding what motivates individuals with diabetes is central to improving self-compliance.

Intrinsic vs Extrinsic Motivation
Intrinsic motivation, which comes from within, often leads to more sustainable self-compliance. This might include pursuing a healthier lifestyle because it aligns with personal values or a desire for improved well-being. Extrinsic motivation, driven by external rewards or punishments, can work but may be less effective in the long term. Thus, doing something because you believe in it is provides sustainable compliance, rather than doing it because you may receive something for it.

Maintaining Motivation
Motivation can fluctuate over time. It's essential to identify strategies for maintaining motivation, especially during challenging periods. This might involve setting clear goals, finding social support, or rewarding yourself for achievements. Hence, understanding the psychology of self-compliance is a journey into the complexities of human behavior, shedding light on why individuals make certain choices and how to empower them to make healthier ones.

Recognizing and Overcoming Excuses
Excuses often stand as formidable barriers to self-compliance in diabetes management. They are the well-crafted rationalizations that allow us to deviate from our prescribed path. Therefore, to navigate the landscape of diabetes successfully, it's crucial to recognize these excuses for what they are and develop strategies to overcome them.

The Anatomy of Excuses
Excuses are cleverly designed justifications that we present to ourselves or others to rationalize non-compliance with our diabetes management plans. They often sound reasonable on the surface but can lead to detrimental consequences for our health.

Common Excuses
Excuses in diabetes management can take various forms. Some of the most common ones include:

"I'm too busy." - The fast pace of modern life often leads to the excuse of being too busy to prioritize self-care.

"It's too hard." - The complexity of managing diabetes can make it seem daunting, leading to the belief that it's too difficult to adhere to recommendations.

"Just this once won't hurt." - This excuse allows for occasional deviations from the dietary plan, which can accumulate over time.

"I deserve a treat." - Using food as a reward can be a comforting but detrimental excuse for non-compliance.

"I'll start tomorrow." - Procrastination is the most significant of common excuses. People often put off adherence until some unspecified future date.

Self-Compliance and Avoiding Excuses

The Impact of Excuses
Excuses are not harmless. They have real consequences. Each time we succumb to an excuse, we disrupt the consistency of our self-care routines. This can lead to fluctuating blood glucose levels, increased risk of complications, and a sense of frustration and guilt.

Consider the "just this once" excuse. While indulging occasionally may not seem harmful, it can easily become a pattern that compromises long-term adherence. Over time, these small deviations can contribute to less stable blood glucose control and undermine the effectiveness of treatment.

Recognizing Excuses
The first step in overcoming excuses is to recognize them. Excuses often hide in plain sight, masquerading as legitimate reasons for non-compliance. To identify them, practice self-awareness and reflection.

Journaling
Keeping a journal of your daily actions and decisions related to diabetes management, or really anything, can be enlightening.

- Note instances when you deviate from your diabetes management plan and the reasons behind these deviations.

Over time, patterns of excuses may emerge.

Seeking Feedback
Engaging with a primary care provider, licensed dietitian-nutritionist, or diabetes educator, or a trusted friend or family member can provide an external perspective. They can help you recognize excuses you might be overlooking.

Strategies for Overcoming Excuses
Once you've identified excuses, it's essential to develop strategies for overcoming them. Remember, you have the power to choose your health over excuses. Therefore, this guide provided some effective strategies for conquering excuses and learning to become more transparent.

Create a Plan
Develop a clear and realistic diabetes management plan that includes specific actions and goals. Having a structured plan reduces room for excuses.

Visualize Success
Imagine the positive outcomes of adhering to your plan. Visualization can enhance motivation and reduce the temptation of excuses.

Accountability
Share your goals and progress with a trusted friend, family member, primary care provider, or licensed dietitian-nutritionist. Knowing that someone is monitoring your adherence can deter excuses.

Problem-Solving
When faced with a situation that triggers an excuse, engage in problem-solving. Instead of succumbing to the excuse, find creative solutions to maintain compliance.

Practice Self-Compassion
Be kind to yourself. Recognize that occasional slips are normal, and self-criticism only fuels excuses. Treat setbacks as opportunities to learn and grow.

The Empowerment of Excuse-Free Living
Overcoming excuses is not about perfection; it's about progress and empowerment. Excuse-free living in diabetes management means acknowledging the challenges but choosing to prioritize your health anyway. It means embracing a mindset of resilience and determination. By recognizing and conquering excuses, you take control of your health journey. You free yourself from the limitations of rationalizations and step into a world of self-empowerment.

Building a Supportive Network for Accountability
The Importance of Accountability
Accountability is a powerful force in diabetes management, but it's not a burden to bear alone. The journey becomes more manageable and fulfilling when you build a supportive network around you. This network acts as a safety net, thereby providing encouragement, understanding, and shared responsibility for your well-being. Thus, accountability goes beyond a sense of obligation, it's a collaborative effort to achieve common goals. For diabetes management, accountability plays a pivotal role in maintaining consistency and adherence to your new health journey and diabetes management plan. It helps you stay on track when faced with challenges and empowers you to make informed decisions. If you have a supportive network, you'll likely stay on your path leading to successful lifestyle transformation.

Consider this example, a scenario where you've set a goal to eat a salad daily. Having an accountability partner can make all the difference. This is an alliance or collaboration. When you share your progress with someone who genuinely cares about your health, you're more likely to stick to your routine and address any lapses promptly because you support each other.

Building Your Supportive Network

Creating a supportive network for accountability involves identifying and engaging with individuals who can contribute to your health journey. Here are key components of this network:

Healthcare Team
Your primary care provider, licensed dietitian-nutritionist, or diabetes educator are essential members of your support network. They provide expert guidance, monitor your progress, and adjust your treatment plan as needed. Regular appointments and open communication are vital.

Family and Friends
Loved ones play a central role in your support network. Their encouragement, understanding, and willingness to accommodate your health needs can significantly impact your adherence. Share your goals and challenges with them, allowing them to be part of your journey.

Support Groups
Consider joining a diabetes support group in your community or online. These groups provide a platform to connect with others facing similar challenges. Sharing experiences, insights, and strategies can be empowering and reassuring.

Accountability Partners
Choose a trusted friend or family member to be your accountability partner. This person can help you stay on track with your goals, remind you of appointments, and offer emotional support when needed.

Effective Communication

Effective communication is at the heart of a supportive network. Here are some guidelines for fostering open and productive communication:

Be Honest
Share your experiences, challenges, and successes openly with your network. Honesty is essential for receiving relevant support.

Express Your Needs
Clearly communicate your needs and expectations from your support network. For example, if you need reminders or assistance with meal planning, don't hesitate to ask for help.

Listen Actively
Listening to the experiences and advice of others in your network can provide valuable insights. Be receptive to their input while making informed decisions that align with your diabetes management plan.

Shared Responsibility
Accountability doesn't mean transferring responsibility for your health to others. Instead, it's about shared responsibility. You remain the captain of your health journey, making decisions about your care. However, your support network shares the voyage with you, providing guidance, motivation, and encouragement along the way.

Celebrating Successes and Learning from Setbacks
In a supportive network, successes are celebrated, and setbacks are viewed as opportunities for growth. Recognize and appreciate the achievements, no matter how small they may seem. Likewise, learn from setbacks, using them as stepping stones toward improved self-care.

Prioritizing Self-Care and Saying No

Putting Yourself First: Why It Matters

It's easy to find oneself caught in the rhythm of external demands and obligations. For those navigating the challenges of diabetes, this can be particularly taxing. However, it's crucial to recognize that putting yourself first is not an act of selfishness but a profound act of self-care and self-preservation. In this chapter, we explore why putting yourself first matters in the context of diabetes management.

The Myth of Selfishness

Before getting into the importance of putting yourself first, let's dispel a common myth, the belief that prioritizing your well-being is a selfish act. In reality, it's quite the opposite. By prioritizing your health and self-care, you ensure that you are in the best possible condition to fulfill your responsibilities and support others effectively.

Imagine a scenario where you constantly put the needs of others ahead of your own, neglecting the management of your condition in the process. Over time, this neglect can lead to worsening health, reduced energy, and increased stress. Your ability to care for others may become compromised, and the quality of your relationships may suffer.

The Oxygen Mask Analogy

The analogy of the oxygen mask on an airplane is a great way to put things into perspective. Consider this. In the event of an emergency, flight attendants instruct passengers to secure their own masks before assisting others, including children or those in need. This seemingly counterintuitive advice has a profound underlying wisdom. Hence, if you are not well, you cannot effectively help others.

Similarly, in the journey of managing diabetes, securing your "oxygen mask" by prioritizing your health allows you to be present, capable, and resilient in your roles as a partner, parent, friend, or caregiver. It's a fundamental act of self-preservation that ultimately benefits both you and those you care about.

Physical and Emotional Well-Being

Putting yourself first encompasses both physical and emotional well-being. This means adhering to prescribed diets and treatments, adopting a healthier lifestyle, and proactively addressing emotional health.

Physical Well-Being
Prioritizing physical well-being involves adhering to diet recommendations

first, medication regimens to support dietary methods, and exercise routines to filter medications through the system. It means scheduling regular check-ups and monitoring blood glucose levels consistently. These actions are not selfish; they are essential for your health and longevity.

Emotional Well-Being
Diabetes can take an emotional toll. Managing the condition often involves stress, anxiety, and occasional feelings of frustration or guilt. Prioritizing your emotional well-being means seeking support, whether through therapy, counseling, or support groups. It means acknowledging your feelings and taking steps to address them rather than bottling them up.

The Ripple Effect of Self-Care
When you put yourself first in the context of diabetes management, you set in motion a positive ripple effect. Your self-care actions influence not only your health but also those around you. Consider the following ways in which self-care impacts others:

Inspiration
Your commitment to self-care can inspire loved ones to prioritize their health as well. Your actions set an example that others may follow.

Reduced Stress
When you are in better health, those who care about you experience reduced stress and worry. They can focus on supporting you rather than being consumed by concerns about your well-being.

Quality Time
By managing your diabetes effectively, you increase the quality of the time you spend with loved ones. You can fully engage in activities and conversations, free from the distractions of uncontrolled symptoms.

Longevity
Prioritizing self-care can lead to a longer, healthier life, allowing you to be present for significant milestones in the lives of those you care about.

The Empowerment of Self-Care
Putting yourself first in diabetes management is not a selfish act; it's an empowering one. It's a declaration that your health and well-being matter and deserve attention. It's a commitment to be the best version of yourself, not only for your sake but also for the sake of those you love.

Strategies for Saying No Without Guilt

Learning to say "no" is a vital thread, and it becomes even more crucial when managing a chronic condition like diabetes. Saying no isn't about being uncooperative; it's about prioritizing your health and well-being. However, it's often accompanied by feelings of guilt or the fear of disappointing others. In this section, we explore strategies to say no gracefully, assertively, and without guilt.

Understanding the Guilt Trap

Let's examine why this emotion often accompanies refusal. Guilt can arise from several sources:

Social Expectations
Society often places a strong emphasis on being accommodating and selfless. Saying no can feel like deviating from these expectations.

Fear of Disappointment
We may fear disappointing or letting down others, especially when we care about their well-being or approval.

Desire for Connection
Human beings have an innate desire for connection and belonging. Saying no can sometimes feel like a rejection of these fundamental needs.

Prior Conditioning
Past experiences and cultural conditioning can shape our responses. If we've been raised to prioritize the needs of others over our own, saying no may feel uncomfortable.

The Importance of Boundaries

Effective communication and setting clear boundaries are at the core of saying no without guilt. Boundaries define the limits of what you are comfortable with and willing to accept. Establishing and maintaining healthy boundaries is a fundamental aspect of self-care.

Recognize Your Limits
Begin by identifying your physical, emotional, and time limits. Understanding what you can realistically handle is the first step in setting boundaries.

Practice Self-Awareness
Tune into your feelings and emotions when requests are made. If saying yes

feels like a burden or compromises your well-being, it's a signal to set a boundary.

Be Assertive, Not Aggressive
Saying no assertively means communicating your decision respectfully and clearly without aggression or hostility. Use "I" statements to express your feelings and needs.

Strategies for Saying No Without Guilt
Polite Firmness
You can say no politely and firmly without the need for elaborate explanations. For example, "I appreciate the invitation, but I need to prioritize my health right now."

Empathetic Decline
Express understanding and empathy while declining. This shows that you respect the other person's request but have valid reasons for saying no. For example, "I understand the importance of this event, but I have a prior commitment."

Offer Alternatives
If possible, provide alternatives or compromises that align with your boundaries. This can demonstrate your willingness to find a solution. For example, "I can't attend the entire meeting, but I can contribute by reviewing the notes afterward."

Buy Time
If you need to consider a request, it's acceptable to buy time before giving an answer. This allows you to evaluate whether the commitment aligns with your priorities. For example, "Let me check my schedule and get back to you tomorrow."

Practice Self-Compassion
Recognize that saying no is an act of self-care, not selfishness. Treat yourself with the same kindness and understanding that you extend to others.

Handling Reactions
It's natural to anticipate reactions when you say no, but remember that you are not responsible for the feelings or responses of others. Some may understand and respect your boundaries, while others may express

disappointment or frustration.

Stay Calm and Confident
Maintain your composure and confidence in your decision. Avoid apologizing excessively or justifying your choices.

Empathize and Listen
If the other person is upset or disappointed, empathize with their feelings and listen actively. Offer reassurance and understanding.

Stand Firm
If the requestor persists or attempts to pressure you into changing your decision, politely but firmly reiterate your boundaries.

Balancing Responsibilities and Self-Care
Balancing the demands of everyday life while managing diabetes can often feel like walking a tightrope, juggling glass balls. Responsibilities, whether they involve work, family, or personal commitments, can sometimes take precedence, leaving self-care teetering on the edge. At times, it may seem like a relentless juggling act, and dropping any of these balls can have shattering consequences. However, it's essential to recognize that the teetering health of your life is out of balance, and if neglected for too long, it can fall over the edge affecting not only you but also any of the other aspects of your life, creating a failing act.

The Myth of Perfection
One of the biggest obstacles to balancing responsibilities and self-care is the myth of perfection. Many individuals with diabetes feel an immense pressure to manage their condition flawlessly. They believe that any deviation from their prescribed regimen is a failure. In reality, perfection is an unattainable goal, and the pursuit of it can lead to stress, burnout, and a diminished quality of life. Balancing responsibilities and self-care is not about perfection; it's about finding a sustainable equilibrium that supports your overall well-being.

Prioritizing Self-Care
To strike a balance between responsibilities and self-care, it's essential to prioritize self-care as a non-negotiable component of your daily routine.

Set Clear Boundaries
Establish boundaries that protect your self-care time. Communicate these

boundaries to those around you, so they understand when you need to prioritize your health.

Prioritize Health Appointments
Schedule medical appointments and self-care activities as you would any other important commitment. Treat them with the same level of urgency and importance.

Practice Time Management
Efficient time management can free up valuable moments for self-care. Organize your schedule to maximize productivity, allowing for dedicated self-care time.

Delegate and Seek Support
Don't hesitate to delegate tasks or ask for support when needed. Enlist the help of family members, friends, or colleagues to lighten your load.

Embracing Flexibility
Flexibility is key to maintaining equilibrium. Life is dynamic, and unexpected challenges or opportunities may arise. When faced with changes to your routine, adapt and modify your self-care plan as needed. For instance, if work responsibilities suddenly increase, you may need to adjust your exercise routine or meal planning. Thus, if your workplace is an environment that involves physical movement, like a moving company or restaurant, then perhaps you can utilize your work atmosphere for exercise rather than trying to squeeze in a trip at a gym. Logging you steps as you walk through your kitchen or lifting more than usual can take precedence over certain exercises at the gym. Flexibility does not mean compromising your self-care but finding creative ways to integrate it into shifting circumstances.

Stress Management
Stress is a common companion in the pursuit of balancing responsibilities and self-care. Chronic stress can have adverse effects on blood glucose levels and overall health. Therefore, it's crucial to develop effective stress management techniques, such as walking, yoga or tai chi, cooking, cleaning, meditation, deep breathing exercises, or mindfulness.

Seeking Professional Guidance
Navigating the balance between responsibilities and self-care can be challenging. If you find it particularly daunting or overwhelming, consider seeking the guidance of a primary care provider, licensed

dietitian-nutritionist, or diabetes educator. They can help tailor a self-care plan that aligns with your unique circumstances and responsibilities.

The Reward of Balance
Balancing responsibilities and self-care is not a one-size-fits-all endeavor. It's a personalized journey that requires self-awareness, adaptability, and commitment. However, the reward is a life that is not only well-managed in terms of diabetes but also fulfilling in all its facets.

Navigating Medical Advice

Common Misconceptions About Diabetes Treatment

Misconceptions can cloud the path to effective treatment. These misunderstandings, often rooted in outdated information or myths, can hinder progress and lead to suboptimal outcomes. In this chapter, we debunk some of the most common misconceptions about diabetes treatment, shedding light on the truth to empower individuals to make informed decisions about their health.

Misconception 1: "Diabetes is a Disease of the Elderly"

One prevalent misconception about diabetes is that it exclusively affects older adults. While it's true that the risk of developing diabetes increases with age, diabetes can and does occur in individuals of all ages, including children and young adults. This misconception can delay diagnosis and treatment in younger individuals, potentially leading to complications.

Misconception 2: "Insulin is the Last Resort"

Many individuals with diabetes fear insulin therapy and believe it is only used when other treatments fail. While insulin may be introduced later in the treatment plan for some individuals, it is not a last resort. Insulin can be a highly effective and necessary treatment option, even for those with type 2 diabetes. It should not be delayed when needed to achieve optimal blood glucose control.

Misconception 3: "You Can Feel High or Low Blood Sugar"

Another common misconception is that individuals with diabetes can always feel when their blood glucose is too high or too low. While some people may experience symptoms, such as thirst or dizziness, many do not exhibit noticeable signs. Relying on symptoms alone is not a reliable method for blood glucose management. Regular monitoring is essential.

Misconception 4: Natural Remedies Can't Cure Diabetes"

Some individuals believe that medication is the only way to reverse diabetes, and this is often stated to them by their practitioners. However, there's a powerful truth that dietary changes can significantly improve and even reverse Type 2 diabetes. While it is well-established that lifestyle modifications, including diet and exercise, can have a profound impact on managing this condition, it's crucial to understand the potential for positive change.

Type 2 diabetes is often characterized by insulin resistance and impaired glucose metabolism. Lifestyle changes, such as adopting a healthy diet and increasing physical activity, can lead to remarkable improvements in blood glucose control. In some cases, individuals can achieve a state where blood glucose levels return to within the normal range. This is often referred to as reversing Type 2 diabetes.

It's important to note that the term "reversal" implies that the underlying factors contributing to Type 2 diabetes have been addressed to the point where the condition no longer requires medication or active management. While sustaining these dietary changes is crucial for maintaining this positive outcome, the potential for lasting improvement is real. Therefore, dietary changes can indeed lead to the reversal of Type 2 diabetes, providing individuals with an opportunity to regain control of their health without relying on medication. Maintaining these dietary habits is the key to long-term success and continued well-being.

Misconception 5: "Dietary Choices Don't Matter if You Take Medications"
This misconception assumes that diabetes medications can compensate for poor dietary choices. While medications can help manage blood glucose levels, they are most effective when combined with a healthy diet. Dietary choices play a crucial role in diabetes management, affecting blood glucose control, weight management, and overall well-being.

The Power of Knowledge
Dispelling these misconceptions is a vital step in diabetes education and empowerment. Knowledge is a powerful tool that enables individuals to make informed decisions about their treatment and lifestyle. By understanding the truth about diabetes and its management, individuals can take charge of their health and work collaboratively with healthcare professionals to achieve optimal outcomes.

Questioning Doctors' Recommendations: When and How
Doctors play a critical role in diabetes management, providing guidance, prescriptions, and treatment plans. However, it's essential for individuals with diabetes to be active participants in their healthcare journey, including knowing when to question doctors' recommendations to ensure that their treatment plan aligns with their unique needs and preferences.

The Importance of Advocacy
Diabetes management is not a one-size-fits-all endeavor. Each individual's experience with the condition is unique, influenced by factors such as age,

lifestyle, co-existing health conditions, and personal preferences. To receive the most appropriate care, individuals must become advocates for their own health. Questioning doctors' recommendations is not about challenging their expertise but about collaborating as a team to make informed decisions. Advocacy ensures that the treatment plan is tailored to the individual, maximizing its effectiveness.

When to Question Doctors' Recommendations
When You Don't Understand
If a doctor provides recommendations or instructions that you do not fully comprehend, it is entirely appropriate to seek clarification. Understanding the "why" behind a recommendation is essential for compliance and informed decision-making.

When You Have Concerns
If you have concerns about a proposed treatment, medication, or test, discuss them with your doctor. These concerns may be related to potential side effects, cost, or the impact on your daily life. For instance, if your doctor advises against consuming certain healthy foods, and you find this advice puzzling, don't hesitate to seek clarification. You may have valid reasons to question this advice. You might suspect that a particular food item has a faster impact on blood glucose levels, potentially exacerbating high blood glucose reactions rather than improving them. In such situations, asking questions is not only acceptable but encouraged. It allows you to gain a deeper understanding of the reasoning behind the recommendations and empowers you to make informed decisions about your health.

When You Seek Alternatives
If you are interested in exploring alternative treatments, lifestyle modifications, or complementary therapies, discuss these options with your doctor. They can provide insights and guide you toward evidence-based choices.

When Your Goals Differ
It's important to align your treatment goals with your doctor's recommendations. If your goals differ from the proposed treatment plan (e.g., you prioritize lifestyle changes or diet over medication), express your preferences and discuss how they can be integrated into the plan.

How to Question Doctors' Recommendations
Effective communication is key when questioning doctors'

recommendations. Here are some strategies for constructive dialogue:

Be Respectful
Approach the conversation with respect for your doctor's expertise and experience. Avoid confrontational or adversarial language.

Ask Open-Ended Questions
Encourage discussion by asking open-ended questions, such as "Can you explain the reasoning behind this recommendation?" or "What are the potential benefits and risks?"

Express Your Concerns
Clearly articulate your concerns or preferences. Use "I" statements to convey your thoughts and feelings. For example, "I have reservations about taking this medication due to potential side effects."

Seek a Second Opinion
If you have significant doubts or if your goals are not aligned with your current doctor's recommendations, consider seeking a second opinion from another healthcare professional.

Request Additional Information
If you require more information or research to make an informed decision, ask your doctor for relevant resources or studies that support their recommendation.

The Patient-Practitioner Relationship
Collaboration between practitioners and patients is a fundamental aspect of effective healthcare. Practitioners value patients who actively engage in their care, ask questions, and express their concerns. This partnership enhances the quality of care and contributes to better health outcomes.

It's important to remember that doctors (medical practitioners), differ from other practitioners. Their practice is built around prescribing medications. While, for example, a licensed dietitian-nutritionist is built around prescribing diet and lifestyle. Every practitioner has their niche that they deeply value and believe in. Both principles work, nonetheless, may work even better when combined in practice. Doctors, however, are not infallible, and treatment plans may evolve over time based on your response and changing circumstances. Regular communication about how you'd like your health treated and a willingness to adapt are essential components of this partnership.

The Empowerment of Informed Decisions
Questioning doctors' recommendations is not a sign of defiance; it's a demonstration of empowerment and responsibility for one's health. When individuals actively participate in their diabetes management, they are more likely to make informed decisions, adhere to treatment plans, and achieve optimal health outcomes.

Collaborating with Healthcare Professionals for Optimal Care
Effective diabetes management is a collaborative effort between individuals and their practitioners. Building a strong partnership with your healthcare team is essential for achieving and maintaining optimal care.

The Healthcare Team
Your healthcare team consists of various professionals who contribute to your diabetes care and they are your allies in diabetes management. This team typically includes:

Primary Care Physician
Your first point of contact for diabetes management is usually your doctor, who may refer you to specialists as needed. They may work independently or with licensed dietitian-nutritionist, diabetes educator, endocrinologist, or mental health practitioner.

Licensed Dietitian-Nutritionist or Diabetes Educator
Some seek differing practitioners that are fluent in their disease. An licensed dietitian-nutritionist or diabetes educator is a healthcare professional with specialized knowledge in diabetes education, who can help you understand and manage your diabetes, who is also an expert in nutrition who can assist with meal planning and dietary choices tailored to your diabetes needs.

Endocrinologist
A specialist in diabetes care who can provide in-depth expertise in managing the condition through medication and specialized services involving in-depth knowledge of how the endocrine system works during the presence of this condition. They may work independently or with licensed dietitian-nutritionist or diabetes educator.

Principles of Collaboration
Collaboration with healthcare professionals is built on several key principles:

Open Communication
Maintain open and honest communication with your healthcare team. Share your concerns, goals, and experiences openly.

Shared Decision-Making
Engage in shared decision-making. Discuss treatment options, set goals, and make decisions together with your practitioners.

Active Participation
Be an active participant in your care. Take responsibility for adhering to treatment plans, monitoring your health, and reporting any changes or concerns.

Mutual Respect
Show respect for the expertise of your practitioners, and expect the same respect in return.

Regular Follow-Up
Schedule and attend regular follow-up appointments to monitor your progress and make necessary adjustments to your care plan.

Practical Strategies for Collaboration

Prepare for Appointments
Before appointments, write down questions or concerns you want to address. Bring a record of your blood glucose readings, medication lists, and any changes in your health.

Express Your Goals
Share your goals and priorities with your healthcare team. Whether it's achieving specific blood glucose targets or making lifestyle changes, clear goals help guide your care.

Follow Recommendations
Adhere to the recommendations provided by your healthcare team. This includes taking medications as prescribed, monitoring your blood glucose regularly, and making necessary lifestyle changes.

Collaborate on Adjustments
If your treatment plan needs adjustment due to changing circumstances or challenges, work collaboratively with your healthcare provider to find solutions.

Seek Clarification
If you receive recommendations or instructions that you don't fully understand, ask for clarification. Your healthcare team is there to help you.

Building Trust
Trust is a foundational element of the doctor-patient relationship. Building and maintaining trust with your healthcare providers can enhance the quality of care you receive. Trust is fostered through open communication, shared decision-making, and consistent collaboration.

The Benefits of Collaboration
Collaborating with your healthcare providers has numerous benefits:

Optimal Health Outcomes
Effective collaboration helps you achieve and maintain optimal blood glucose control, reducing the risk of complications.

Empowerment
Active participation in your care empowers you to make informed decisions and take charge of your health.

Better Problem-Solving
When challenges arise, collaboration enables you and your healthcare team to work together to find effective solutions.

Improved Quality of Life
With optimal care and support, you can enjoy a higher quality of life, both physically and emotionally.

Research and Understanding Diabetes

Unpacking the Types and Causes of Diabetes

Diabetes is a complex and diverse group of chronic conditions that affect millions of individuals worldwide. Understanding the various types of diabetes and their underlying causes is essential for both prevention and effective management.

Diabetes is not a one-size-fits-all condition; it exists on a spectrum, encompassing different types and variations. The four primary types of diabetes are:

Type 1 Diabetes (Autoimmune Disease)

This autoimmune condition occurs when the body's immune system mistakenly targets and destroys the insulin-producing beta cells in the pancreas. As a result, individuals with Type 1 diabetes must rely on insulin injections or pumps to manage their blood glucose levels.

The exact cause of Type 1 diabetes remains under investigation, but researchers have found that genetic predisposition, specifically to the HLA genes of the major histocompatibility complex (MHC) that encode genes on the surface of immune cells. Environmental triggers (viral infections) or encoding issues can activate the gene of chromosome 6, which contains HLA class 1 and class 2 molecules. These cells are responsible for telling the body that there is a pathogen present, or instructs the body to destroy the cell because there is a malfunction.

People with type 1 diabetes are usually diagnosed during childhood because the gene is triggered very early in life. Some cases differ, where adult may be triggered later in life.

Type 2 Diabetes (Preventative Disease)

The most common form of diabetes, Type 2 diabetes, is characterized by insulin resistance, where the body's cells do not respond effectively to insulin. Over time, the pancreas may struggle to produce enough insulin to compensate for this resistance. Multiple factors contribute to the development of Type 2 diabetes, including genetics, obesity, physical inactivity, poor diet, and aging.

The misconception, "My Type 2 diabetes is genetic, I can't do nothing to get rid of it," is untrue. Type 2 diabetes is not a genetic disease. It is a preventative condition. Nonetheless, it is true that individuals with a family history of the disease are at a higher risk of developing it themselves.

Researchers have identified specific genetic variants associated with an increased susceptibility to Type 2 diabetes. However, these genetic factors affect how the body processes and responds to insulin itself, and not the attack of the immune system on the cells. The way the body processes and responds to insulin can be redirected with modifications. Such anomalies include lifestyle and dietary changes, such as eating nutrient-dense meals, eliminating smoking and drinking, reducing stress, getting adequate sleep, and adding exercise.

Gestational Diabetes (Hormonal Influence)
Occurring during pregnancy, gestational diabetes affects some women who did not have diabetes before becoming pregnant. Hormonal changes during pregnancy can lead to insulin resistance. While gestational diabetes typically resolves after childbirth, it increases the risk of developing Type 2 diabetes later in life.

Type 3 Diabetes (Alzheimer's Disease)
Emerging research has led to the recognition of a potential link between Alzheimer's disease and diabetes, referred to as Type 3 diabetes. This association underscores the importance of blood glucose regulation not only for metabolic health but also for cognitive well-being. The glucose issue lies in the brain region rather than the body, called 'brain insulin resistance".

The Role of Insulin
Insulin is a hormone produced by the pancreas that plays a central role in regulating blood glucose levels. When you eat, your digestive system breaks down carbohydrates into glucose, a form of sugar that enters the bloodstream. In response, the pancreas releases insulin, which enables
glucose to enter cells for energy or storage.

In Type 1 diabetes, the immune system's attack on beta cells leads to a lack of insulin production. In Type 2 diabetes, the body becomes less responsive to insulin, and the pancreas may struggle to produce enough to maintain normal blood glucose levels; while Type 3 diabetes has insulin resistance in the brain. This disruption in insulin function is a hallmark of all types of diabetes.

The Causes of Type 1 Diabetes
The precise cause of Type 1 diabetes remains an active area of research. It is believed to involve a combination of genetic susceptibility and environmental factors. Some contributing factors include:

Genetic Predisposition
Individuals with a family history of Type 1 diabetes have a higher risk of developing the condition.

Autoimmune Response
It is thought that exposure to certain viruses or other environmental triggers may prompt an autoimmune response in genetically susceptible individuals, leading to the destruction of beta cells.

Environmental Factors
Viral infections and dietary factors have been investigated as potential triggers for Type 1 diabetes, although the exact mechanisms are still being studied.

The Causes of Type 2 Diabetes
Type 2 diabetes is primarily associated with lifestyle and genetic factors. While genetics can predispose individuals to the condition, modifiable factors play a significant role:

Obesity
Excess body weight, particularly abdominal fat, is a strong risk factor for Type 2 diabetes. Obesity contributes to insulin resistance and inflammation.

Physical Inactivity
A sedentary lifestyle reduces insulin sensitivity and increases the risk of Type 2 diabetes.

Poor Diet
Diets high in sugar, unhealthy fats, and processed foods can contribute to obesity and insulin resistance.

Genetic Factors
Family history or age (after 45 years) can influence the risk of Type 2 diabetes when the above mentioned factors are in play, suggesting a genetic component.

Prevention and Management
Understanding the types and causes of diabetes is a major step toward prevention and effective management. Prevention efforts often focus on lifestyle modifications, such as adherence to regimes, self-compliance, self-care, maintaining a healthy weight, engaging in regular physical activity,

and adopting a balanced diet. Effective diabetes management aims to achieve and maintain optimal blood glucose control, reducing the risk of complications and enhancing overall well-being.

Recent Advancements in Diabetes Research

Diabetes research is a dynamic field that continually evolves, driven by the quest to better understand the condition, improve treatment options, and eventually find a cure. Recent research in the field of diabetes has seen exciting developments in various areas, including nutrition, viral influences, and lifestyle interventions. These advancements hold promise for both Type 1 and Type 2 diabetes management.

Potential Vaccine for Type 1 Diabetes

Researchers have been exploring the intriguing possibility of a vaccine that may help prevent or delay the onset of Type 1 diabetes. One avenue of investigation involves viral influences on the development of autoimmune responses. It is suggested that certain viruses may trigger or exacerbate the immune system's attack on insulin-producing beta cells. By understanding these viral influences, scientists are working to develop vaccines that could potentially modulate the immune response and reduce the risk of Type 1 diabetes.

Enteroviruses

Enteroviruses, a group of viruses that includes Coxsackie viruses and echoviruses, have been of particular interest. Studies have shown that individuals with Type 1 diabetes often have a higher prevalence of enterovirus infections or specific antibodies against these viruses. Enteroviruses can infect pancreatic cells, potentially leading to immune system activation and the destruction of beta cells.

Molecular Mimicry

One hypothesis is that viral proteins may resemble proteins found in beta cells. This resemblance can confuse the immune system, causing it to attack both the virus and the beta cells. This phenomenon is known as molecular mimicry and is considered a potential trigger for autoimmunity in Type 1 diabetes.

Role of Gut Microbiome

Emerging research is also exploring the connection between viral infections, the gut microbiome, and Type 1 diabetes. Viruses may influence the composition and function of the gut microbiome, which, in turn, can impact the immune system and autoimmunity.

Lifestyle Change Methods for Type 2 Diabetes
Lifestyle modifications are at the forefront of Type 2 diabetes management. Recent research emphasizes the importance of comprehensive lifestyle changes, including:

- Nutritional methods
- Physical activity
- Reducing intake of alcohol
- Stress management
- Adequate quality sleep
- Eliminating smoking

These holistic approaches aim to address the root causes of insulin resistance and metabolic dysfunction, allowing for better long-term management of the condition. In the next chapters we dive into exercise and nutritional methods and the latest research involving diabetes..

The Future of Diabetes Treatment and Prevention
The landscape of diabetes treatment and prevention is continually evolving, driven by innovative research, advanced technologies, and a growing understanding of this complex condition. The future of diabetes care depends upon the exploration of promising avenues for treatment, prevention, and the potential to transform the lives of individuals affected by diabetes.

Preventive Lifestyle Education
Education on healthy lifestyles remains a cornerstone of diabetes prevention and management. Future initiatives will likely emphasize the importance of preventive education, offering individuals the knowledge and skills to make informed choices about nutrition, physical activity, stress management, and sleep. These education programs will empower people to take proactive steps to reduce their diabetes risk.

Biomarker Discovery for Early Detection
Early detection of diabetes and prediabetes is crucial for timely intervention. Future research aims to identify biomarkers, indicators in the body that can signal the risk or presence of diabetes. These biomarkers may include specific molecules in the blood, genetic markers, or even digital health data from wearable devices. Early detection allows for prompt intervention and

lifestyle modifications.

Personalized Diabetes Therapies
Advances in genetics and personalized medicine are leading to tailored approaches for diabetes management. Personalized therapies may involve customized medication regimens, diet plans, and exercise prescriptions based on an individual's genetic makeup, metabolic profile, and response to treatment.

Labs used for personalized therapy are:
- HbA1c
- Fasting blood glucose
- Fasting blood insulin
- HOMA-IR
- C-Peptide
- Lipid Profile
- eGFR
- Comprehensive metabolic panel
- Urinalysis

Specialized Tools used for personalized therapy are:
- Micronutrient tests
  - Chromium
  - Vitamin D
  - Magnesium
  - Zinc
  - Glutathione
- Food sensitivity testing
- Glycemic index testing
- Gut microbiome testing
- Nutrigenomic testing

This approach ensures more effective and personalized care.

Licensed Dietitian-Nutritionist Visits and Their Importance
Integrating nutrition practitioners, such as registered dietitians and medical nutritionist specialists, into diabetes care teams is becoming increasingly important. These professionals play a vital role in helping individuals with diabetes or at risk of diabetes make dietary choices that align with their specific needs and goals. Regular visits with licensed dietitian-nutritionist practitioners provide ongoing support and guidance in achieving and

maintaining a healthy diet.

Collaboration and Multidisciplinary Care
The future of diabetes care is marked by collaboration among healthcare providers, researchers, technology experts, and individuals living with diabetes. Multidisciplinary care teams can offer holistic support that addresses the physical, emotional, and psychological aspects of diabetes. This collaborative approach fosters innovation, ensuring that advancements in research and technology translate into practical solutions for individuals with diabetes.

Exercise and Blood Glucose Regulation

The Role of Exercise in Diabetes Management

Exercise is a powerful tool of diabetes management. It offers a multitude of benefits, from improving blood glucose control to enhancing overall well-being. Exercise plays a vital role in addressing diabetes for several reasons:

Blood Glucose Regulation
Physical activity helps lower blood glucose levels by increasing the body's sensitivity to insulin. It allows glucose to enter cells more effectively, reducing its concentration in the bloodstream.

Weight Management
Regular exercise contributes to weight loss or maintenance, which is crucial for those with diabetes, particularly type 2 diabetes. Excess weight can exacerbate insulin resistance.

Heart Health
Exercise strengthens the cardiovascular system, reducing the risk of heart disease, a common complication of diabetes.

Stress Reduction
Physical activity is a natural stress reducer, which can be particularly beneficial for individuals managing the emotional aspects of diabetes.

Improved Mood
Exercise triggers the release of endorphins, often referred to as "feel-good" hormones, promoting a positive mood and reducing symptoms of depression or anxiety that can accompany diabetes.

Types of Exercise for Diabetes

There are three primary types of exercise that benefit diabetes management:

Aerobic Exercise
This includes activities that elevate your heart rate and breathing, such as brisk walking, jogging, swimming, cycling, and dancing. Aerobic exercise helps improve insulin sensitivity and lower blood glucose levels.

Strength Training
Also known as resistance or weight training, this type of exercise focuses on building muscle. Increased muscle mass can improve insulin action, helping

Exercise and Blood Glucose Regulation

control blood sugar.

Flexibility and Balance
Activities like yoga and stretching exercises enhance flexibility and balance. They are important for overall well-being and can help reduce the risk of falls, especially in older adults with diabetes.

Exercise Guidelines for Diabetes Management
Before beginning an exercise regimen, it's crucial to consult with your primary care provider, especially if you have any pre-existing health conditions. Once cleared for physical activity, consider these guidelines for effective diabetes management:

Frequency
Aim for at least 150 minutes of moderate-intensity aerobic activity per week, distributed over at least three (3) days. Alternatively, engage in 75 minutes of vigorous-intensity aerobic activity.

Consistency
Consistency is key. Establish a regular exercise routine that you can maintain over time.

Hydration
Stay well-hydrated before, during, and after exercise to prevent dehydration.

Blood Glucose Monitoring
Monitor your blood glucose levels regularly, especially before and after exercise. This helps you understand how physical activity affects your body and allows for adjustments in your diabetes management plan.

Foot Care
Proper foot care is essential for individuals with diabetes. Inspect your feet for any signs of blisters, sores, or injuries, and choose appropriate footwear for exercise.

The Personalized Approach
Remember that the best exercise routine for you is one that you enjoy and can incorporate into your lifestyle. Whether it's walking, swimming, cycling, or dancing, choose activities that bring you joy and keep you motivated. Your healthcare team can help you tailor an exercise plan that fits your unique needs and goals.

Building Muscle to Improve Glycogen Storage
The Role of Glycogen in Blood Glucose Control

Glycogen is like a savings account for glucose, serving as an essential buffer against fluctuations in blood glucose levels. When you consume carbohydrates, your body converts them into glucose, which circulates in the bloodstream and provides energy for various bodily functions. However, excess glucose is stored as glycogen in the liver and muscles, ready to be released when needed. When blood glucose drops between meals or during physical activity, the body can break down glycogen and release glucose to maintain stability. This mechanism is particularly crucial for individuals with diabetes, as it helps prevent low blood glucose and provides energy during exercise.

Building Muscle and Glycogen Storage

Muscles play a pivotal role in glycogen storage. The more muscle mass you have, the larger your glycogen reservoirs can be, enhancing your body's ability to regulate blood glucose effectively. Here's how the process works:

Exercise
When you engage in physical activity, especially resistance or strength training exercises, you stimulate the muscles to grow and adapt. This process requires energy, primarily in the form of glucose.

Glycogen Utilization
As your muscles work during exercise, they draw on glycogen stores for immediate energy. This helps prevent spikes in blood glucose levels during physical activity.

Post-Exercise Replenishment
After exercise, your muscles are primed to replenish their glycogen stores. This process continues even after your workout is over, helping stabilize blood glucose levels for hours.

Long-Term Benefits
Over time, consistent exercise and muscle growth lead to increased glycogen storage capacity. This means your body becomes more efficient at storing and utilizing glucose, contributing to better blood glucose control.

Exercise Strategies for Building Muscle

To harness the benefits of muscle for improved glycogen storage and blood glucose regulation, consider these exercise strategies:

Resistance Training
Incorporate resistance training exercises into your routine. This includes activities like weightlifting, bodyweight exercises, and resistance bands. These exercises target specific muscle groups and promote muscle growth.

Progressive Overload
Plan how you'll progress over time. Gradually increase the intensity, duration, complexity, or resistance of your workouts to continually challenge your muscles and promote growth. Progressive overload is a key principle in muscle development.

Variety
Include a variety of exercises to target different muscle groups. This helps ensure balanced muscle development and reduces the risk of overuse injuries.

Nutrition
Support muscle growth with a balanced diet that provides adequate protein and carbohydrates. Protein is crucial for muscle repair and growth, while carbohydrates contribute to glycogen replenishment.

Balancing Exercise and Blood Sugar
Individuals with diabetes must be mindful of blood glucose levels during exercise. Here are some tips for managing blood glucose effectively:

Carbohydrate and Hydration Intake
Depending on the duration and intensity of your workout, you may need to adjust both your carbohydrate and water intake. Some individuals benefit from consuming a small amount of macronutrients before or during exercise to prevent low blood sugar, while others need more.

Recovery
Pay attention to post-exercise recovery because muscles need time to repair and grow. Adequate rest, nutrition, and glycogen replenishment are essential for muscle maintenance.

Creating an Effective Exercise Routine
Opting to have an exercise journey to manage diabetes is a commendable decision. However, the success of your efforts hinges on the design and consistency of your exercise routine. An effective exercise routine is a well-structured plan that considers various elements to maximize its

benefits. Listed are essential building blocks to consider:

Exercise Type
Choose exercises that align with your goals. Include a mix of aerobic (cardiovascular), strength training (resistance), and flexibility/balance exercises to achieve a balanced fitness profile.

Frequency
Determine how often you'll exercise. Consistency is key, so aim for regular workouts. Beginners might start with 3-4 days a week and gradually increase frequency.

Duration
Decide how long each workout will last. The duration may vary depending on the type of exercise and your fitness level. For aerobic exercises, a common goal is 30-60 minutes per session.

Intensity
Intensity refers to the level of effort exerted during exercise. You can measure it using methods like heart rate, perceived exertion, or specific intensity zones. Adjust intensity to match your goals, whether it's building muscle, improving endurance, or enhancing cardiovascular health.

Latest Research
During clinical trials on dietary methods for diabetes, some researchers found that when they added a third treatment arm that included exercise, the experimental groups saw a greater improvement compared to only analyzing experimental diet against a control (standard american diet). They reported increased percentages in biomarker improvements including primary and secondary biomarkers, along with decreased weight, BMI, and fat percentages when measuring anthropometrics and improvements in inflammatory markers.

Tailoring Your Routine to Diabetes Management
When creating an exercise routine to manage diabetes, there are specific considerations to keep in mind:

Timing
Consider the timing of your workouts. Some people with diabetes find that exercising after a meal helps prevent drops in blood sugar, while others prefer to exercise in a fasted state. Experiment to discover what works best

for you.

Individual Goals
Tailor your exercise routine to your individual goals. For example, if weight loss is a primary objective, you might focus on a combination of aerobic and strength training exercises. If improving cardiovascular health is a goal, prioritize aerobic exercises.

When designing your exercise routine, set realistic and achievable goals. Avoid overambitious plans that may lead to burnout or injury. Instead, start with manageable goals and progressively challenge yourself as you gain confidence and strength.

Staying Motivated
Maintaining motivation is a common challenge when it comes to exercise. To stay committed to your routine, consider these strategies:

Variety
Keep your workouts interesting by incorporating a variety of exercises. This prevents boredom and plateaus in progress.

Accountability
Share your goals with a friend or family member who can provide support and hold you accountable.

Track Progress
Keep a workout journal or use fitness apps to track your progress. Seeing your improvements can be motivating.

Rewards
Celebrate your achievements with small rewards. For example, treat yourself to a healthy snack or a favorite activity after a successful workout.

Community
Join exercise classes or groups to connect with others who share similar goals. The sense of community can be motivating and enjoyable.

Mindset
Cultivate a positive mindset. Focus on the benefits of exercise, such as improved health, energy, and mood.

Adaptability
Be flexible with your routine. Life may present unexpected challenges or opportunities, and adapting your plan rather than giving up entirely is a valuable skill.

Consulting a Primary Care Provider
Before starting a new exercise routine, especially if you have underlying health conditions, consult with your primary care provider. They can offer guidance on exercise safety and provide recommendations tailored to your specific health needs.

The Paleo Diet for Blood Glucose Regulation

Exploring the Paleo Diet and Its Principles

The Paleo diet, also known as the Paleolithic or Caveman diet, has gained popularity for its emphasis on whole, unprocessed foods and its potential benefits for various aspects of health, including blood glucose management.

A Journey Back in Time

The Paleo diet takes inspiration from the dietary habits of our ancient ancestors who lived during the Paleolithic era, roughly 2.5 million to 10,000 years ago. It is founded on the idea that our bodies are best adapted to the foods our hunter-gatherer ancestors consumed, long before the advent of modern agriculture and ultra-processed foods. The principles of the Paleo diet are rooted in the belief that the human digestive system has not evolved significantly since that time. Proponents argue that by returning to a diet similar to what our ancestors ate, we can promote better health and well-being.

The Core Principles of the Paleo Diet

The Paleo diet centers around several key principles:

Whole Foods
The foundation of the Paleo diet consists of whole, unprocessed foods. This includes lean meats, fish, poultry, eggs, vegetables, fruits, nuts, and seeds.

Exclusion of Ultra-Processed Foods
Ultra-processed foods, including refined sugars, grains, and artificial additives, are largely excluded from the Paleo diet. This means saying goodbye to sugary cereals, pasta, bread, and packaged snacks.

Emphasis on Protein
Protein-rich foods, such as lean meats and fish, are prominent in the Paleo diet. These sources of protein are essential for muscle maintenance and growth. Plant proteins also play a pivotal role in this diet.

Healthy Fats
The diet incorporates healthy fats, primarily from sources like avocados, nuts, seeds, and olives. These fats provide a source of sustained energy.

Reduction of Grains
Grains, including wheat, rice, and corn, are not part of the traditional Paleo diet. This elimination is rooted in the belief that grains can lead to blood glucose spikes and inflammation. Research has now found that Paleolithic

humans consumed grains, but not as often as modern day humans. They ate them seasonally. Thus, reducing grains to a limited amount can be beneficial to reduce blood glucose spikes, while still providing essential nutrients.

Dairy Exclusion
The Paleo diet excludes dairy products. These are ultra-processed foods and were not prevent until about 10,000 years ago when foods became domesticated.

Legumes
Legumes, such as beans and lentils, are also stated to be restricted in the Paleo diet due to concerns about their lectin content and potential digestive issues. However, Paleolithic humans ate a considerable amount of legumes, which also hold a variety of proteins and also slow the carbohydrate absorption, reducing blood glucose spikes. Therefore, these do not need to be eliminated from the diet.

Blood Glucose Management and the Paleo Diet
One of the potential benefits of the Paleo diet, especially for individuals with diabetes or prediabetes, is its focus on whole, low-glycemic foods. By eliminating ultra-processed domesticated foods, the diet may help regulate blood glucose levels more effectively.

Here are ways the Paleo diet may contribute to better blood glucose management:

Reduced Sugar Intake
By eliminating refined sugars and processed foods, the Paleo diet inherently lowers sugar consumption, which is beneficial for blood glucose control.

Improved Insulin Sensitivity
Some studies suggest that the Paleo diet may enhance insulin sensitivity, making it easier for cells to respond to insulin and regulate blood sugar.

Weight Management
Weight loss is often associated with improved blood glucose control. The Paleo diet's focus on whole foods may support weight management goals.

Steady Energy
The combination of protein, healthy fats, and fiber-rich vegetables and fruits

can provide sustained energy, reducing the likelihood of blood glucose spikes and crashes.

Inflammation Reduction
The diet's emphasis on anti-inflammatory foods like fatty fish and vegetables may help reduce systemic inflammation, which is linked to insulin resistance.

Customizing the Paleo Diet
It's important to note that there is no one-size-fits-all approach to the Paleo diet. Some individuals may choose to adapt it to their specific needs and preferences. For example, those with diabetes might need to pay extra attention to carbohydrate intake from fruits and starchy vegetables, while others may include occasional legumes if it aligns with their dietary goals.

The Paleo diet continues to evolve, with variations and interpretations emerging over time. Some individuals adopt a more relaxed approach, allowing for occasional indulgences, while others adhere strictly to the diet's original principles. Ultimately, the suitability of the Paleo diet for blood glucose management varies from person to person.

The Impact of Paleo on Blood Glucose Levels
The Paleo diet's emphasis on whole foods and its avoidance of ultra-processed foods such as dairy, refined sugars and salt has led many to explore its potential benefits for blood glucose management. Let's examine the impact of the Paleo diet on blood glucose levels and how it may play a role in helping individuals with diabetes or prediabetes achieve better glycemic control.

Stabilizing Blood Glucose Through Whole Foods
One of the core tenets of the Paleo diet is the consumption of whole, nutrient-dense foods. By choosing unprocessed sources of carbohydrates, such as vegetables, fruits, and nuts, individuals on the Paleo diet often experience more stable blood glucose levels.

Here's how the Paleo diet can positively affect blood sugar:

Low Glycemic Index
According to recent advances in research, many foods in the Paleo diet have a low glycemic index (GI) of ≤ 50. This means they are digested and absorbed more slowly, leading to gradual increases in blood glucose rather

than sharp spikes. Low-GI foods include non-starchy vegetables like leafy greens, berries, and nuts.

Biomarkers
Pooled research from 4 systematic reviews and various Paleo diet studies show improved biomarkers for fasting glucose, fasting insulin, hemoglobin A1c, homeostatic model assessment for insulin resistance (HOMA-IR), cardiovascular and lipid biomarkers such as blood pressure, total cholesterol, low-density lipoproteins (LDL), high-density lipoproteins (HDL), and triglycerides after consuming the Paleo diet for 2-12 weeks. Major improvements are shown in individuals who adopt the lifestyle permanently..

Fiber-Rich Choices
Fiber is abundant in Paleo-friendly foods like vegetables, fruits, and nuts that are often consumed when living this way. Legumes for example are high in fiber. Fiber slows down the digestion of carbohydrates, promoting steady blood glucose levels and reducing the risk of post-meal spikes.

Weight Management and Blood Glucose Control
Weight management plays a crucial role in blood glucose control, particularly for individuals with Type 2 diabetes or prediabetes. The Paleo diet's emphasis on whole foods and avoidance of processed sugars and grains may support weight loss and maintenance. Here's how weight management and blood glucose control are interconnected:

Reduced Caloric Density
Research has found that many foods in the Paleo diet are lower in caloric density. During studies, scientist calculated a significant reduction in caloric intake while documenting the same volume of food intake, meaning they provide fewer calories, but people still eat the same amount. This can help individuals consume fewer calories and manage their weight successfully.

Satiety and Appetite Control
During research, scientists found people consuming a Paleo diet felt for satisfied. They reported after thorough evaluation, protein and fiber-rich foods increased after switching over to a Paleo lifestyle. Therefore the Paleo diet promote a sense of fullness in addition to the reduced overall calorie intake. This can prevent overeating and support weight management.

Metabolic Health
Maintaining a healthy weight is associated with improved insulin sensitivity

and better blood glucose control.

Individual Variability and Monitoring
While the Paleo diet can offer substantial benefits for blood glucose management, it's essential to recognize that individual responses vary. Factors like genetics, activity level, and the severity of diabetes or prediabetes can influence how the diet affects blood sugar. To gauge the impact of the Paleo diet on your blood glucose levels, consider the following:

Regular Monitoring
Monitor your blood glucose levels consistently, especially before and after meals. This helps you understand how different foods and meals affect your glucose.

Physical Activity
Complement your dietary changes with regular physical activity. Exercise can help improve insulin sensitivity and enhance blood glucose control.

Medication Adjustments
If you're taking medication or insulin to manage diabetes, be prepared for potential adjustments as your dietary habits change. Consult with your primary care provider to ensure medication doses are appropriate.

Practical Tips for Incorporating Paleo into Your Lifestyle
Transitioning to a Paleo diet can be a rewarding journey, offering the potential for improved health and blood glucose control. In this chapter, we'll explore practical tips and strategies for seamlessly incorporating the principles of the Paleo diet into your daily life, making it a sustainable and enjoyable dietary choice.

1. Start with Small Changes
If the idea of overhauling your entire diet feels overwhelming, don't worry. You can begin by making small, gradual changes. Start by incorporating Paleo-friendly foods and meals into your existing diet. For example, replace your morning cereal with a vegetable and egg scramble or swap your pasta with spiralized zucchini noodles.

2. Educate Yourself
Understanding the principles of the Paleo diet is essential. Familiarize yourself with the types of foods that are allowed and those that should be avoided. Books, online resources, and consultations with registered

dietitians can provide valuable information to support your journey.

3. Plan Your Meals
Meal planning is key to successfully adopting a Paleo diet. Plan your meals for the week, create shopping lists, and prepare ingredients in advance. Having a plan in place reduces the temptation to revert to less healthy options when you're short on time.

4. Explore New Recipes
The Paleo diet can be an exciting culinary adventure. Explore cookbooks, websites, and social media for Paleo-friendly recipes. Experiment with different flavors and ingredients to keep your meals interesting and enjoyable.

5. Embrace Whole Foods
Whole foods should be the cornerstone of your Paleo diet. Fill your plate with a variety of colorful vegetables, lean meats, fatty fish, and fresh fruits. Incorporate nuts, seeds, and healthy fats like olive oil and avocado to enhance flavor and satiety.

6. Be Mindful of Carbohydrates
While the Paleo diet is lower in carbohydrates compared to a standard diet, it still includes carbohydrates from sources like vegetables and fruits. Be mindful of your carbohydrate intake, especially if you're managing blood sugar. Monitor your response to different carbohydrate-rich foods and adjust your choices accordingly.

7. Prioritize Protein
Protein plays a crucial role in the Paleo diet. Include lean meats, poultry, fish, and eggs in your meals. Protein provides a sense of fullness and supports muscle maintenance and growth.

8. Snack Smartly
When snacking on the Paleo diet, choose nutrient-dense options. Snack on raw vegetables with guacamole, a handful of nuts, or a piece of fruit with almond butter. These choices align with the diet's principles and help maintain steady energy levels.

9. Stay Hydrated
Proper hydration is important for overall health. Water is the best choice for hydration, but herbal teas and infused water with slices of fruits or herbs can

add variety to your drinks.

10. Practice Portion Control
While the Paleo diet encourages whole foods, portion control is still essential. Pay attention to your body's hunger and fullness cues, and avoid overeating. Eating mindfully can help prevent excess calorie intake.

11. Customize to Your Needs
Remember that the Paleo diet can be customized to suit your preferences and dietary needs. If you have specific food allergies or sensitivities, adapt the diet accordingly. Work with a licensed dietitian-nutritionist to create a personalized plan.

12. Stay Open to Flexibility
The Paleo diet is not a strict set of rules but a framework for healthier eating. It's okay to occasionally deviate from the diet for special occasions or when dining out. Striving for consistency rather than perfection is key to long-term success.

13. Seek Support
Consider seeking support from others who follow the Paleo diet or have similar health goals. Online communities, local support groups, and social media platforms can provide encouragement, recipes, and advice.

14. Be Patient and Persistent
Adopting any dietary change takes time and persistence. Be patient with yourself and recognize that it's natural to face challenges along the way. Focus on your long-term health goals, and celebrate your successes, no matter how small they may seem.

Incorporating the principles of the Paleo diet into your lifestyle is an empowering step toward better health and blood glucose control. By following these practical tips and staying committed to your goals, you can create a sustainable and enjoyable dietary approach that supports your well-being.

References

References

Boers, I., Muskiet, F. A., Berkelaar, E., Schut, E., Penders, R., Hoenderdos, K., Wichers, H. J., & Jong, M. C. (2014). Favourable effects of consuming a Palaeolithic-type diet on characteristics of the metabolic syndrome: A randomized controlled pilot-study. *Lipids in Health and Disease*, *13*(1), 160. https://doi.org/10.1186/1476-511X-13-160

Challa, H. J., Bandlamudi, M., & Uppaluri, K. R. (2021). Paleolithic Diet. In: *StatPearls*. StatPearls Publishing. https://www.ncbi.nlm.nih.gov/books/NBK482457/

Fontes-Villalba, M., Lindeberg, S., Granfeldt, Y., Knop, F. K., Memon, A. A., Carrera-Bastos, P., Picazo, Ó., Chanrai, M., Sunquist, J., Sundquist, K., & Jönsson, T. (2016). Palaeolithic diet decreases fasting plasma leptin concentrations more than a diabetes diet in patients with type 2 diabetes: A randomized cross-over trial. *Cardiovascular Diabetology*, *15*(1), 80. https://doi.org/10.1186/s12933-016-0398-1

Frassetto, L. A., Shi, L., Schloetter, M., Sebastian, A., & Remer, T. (2013). Established dietary estimates of net acid production do not predict measured net acid excretion in patients with type 2 diabetes on Paleolithic–hunter–gatherer-type diets. *European Journal of Clinical Nutrition*, *67*(9), 899–903. https://doi.org/10.1038/ejcn.2013.124

Gyorkos, A., Baker, M. H., Miutz, L. N., Lown, D. A., Jones, M. A., & Houghton-Rahrig, L. D. (2019). Carbohydrate-restricted diet and high-intensity interval training exercise improve cardio-metabolic and inflammatory profiles in metabolic syndrome: A randomized crossover trial. *Cureus*, *11*(9), e5596. https://doi.org/10.7759/cureus.5596

Jönsson, T., Granfeldt, Y., Ahrén, B., Branell, U.-C., Pålsson, G., Hansson, A., Söderström, M., & Lindeberg, S. (2009). Beneficial effects of a Paleolithic diet on cardiovascular risk factors in type 2 diabetes: A randomized cross-over pilot study. *Cardiovascular Diabetology*, *8*(1), 35. https://doi.org/10.1186/1475-2840-8-35

Jönsson, T., Granfeldt, Y., Erlanson-Albertsson, C., Ahrén, B., & Lindeberg, S. (2010). A paleolithic diet is more satiating per calorie than a mediterranean-like diet in individuals with ischemic heart disease. *Nutrition & Metabolism*, *7*(1), 85. https://doi.org/10.1186/1743-7075-7-85

Jönsson, T., Granfeldt, Y., Lindeberg, S., & Hallberg, A.-C. (2013). Subjective satiety and other experiences of a Paleolithic diet compared to a diabetes diet in patients with type 2 diabetes. *Nutrition Journal*, *12*(1), 105. https://doi.org/10.1186/1475-2891-12-105

References

Mårtensson, A., Stomby, A., Tellström, A., Ryberg, M., Waling, M., & Otten, J. (2021). Using a Paleo ratio to assess adherence to Paleolithic dietary recommendations in a randomized controlled trial of individuals with type 2 diabetes. *Nutrients, 13*(3), 969. https://doi.org/10.3390/nu13030969

Masharani, U., Sherchan, P., Schloetter, M., Stratford, S., Xiao, A., Sebastian, A., Nolte Kennedy, M., & Frassetto, L. (2015). Metabolic and physiologic effects from consuming a hunter-gatherer (Paleolithic)-type diet in type 2 diabetes. *European Journal of Clinical Nutrition, 69*(8), 944–948. https://doi.org/10.1038/ejcn.2015.39

Otten, J., Andersson, J., Ståhl, J., Stomby, A., Saleh, A., Waling, M., Ryberg, M., Hauksson, J., Svensson, M., Johansson, B., & Olsson, T. (2019). Exercise Training Adds Cardiometabolic Benefits of a Paleolithic Diet in Type 2 Diabetes Mellitus. *Journal of the American Heart Association, 8*(2), e010634. https://doi.org/10.1161/JAHA.118.010634

Otten, J., Stomby, A., Waling, M., Isaksson, A., Söderström, I., Ryberg, M., Svensson, M., Hauksson, J., & Olsson, T. (2018). A heterogeneous response of liver and skeletal muscle fat to the combination of a Paleolithic diet and exercise in obese individuals with type 2 diabetes: A randomised controlled trial. *Diabetologia, 61*(7), 1548–1559. https://doi.org/10.1007/s00125-018-4618-y

Otten, J., Stomby, A., Waling, M., Isaksson, A., Tellström, A., Lundin-Olsson, L., Brage, S., Ryberg, M., Svensson, M., & Olsson, T. (2017). Benefits of a Paleolithic diet with and without supervised exercise on fat mass, insulin sensitivity, and glycemic control: A randomized controlled trial in individuals with type 2 diabetes. *Diabetes Metabolism Research and Reviews, 33*(1), 10.1002/dmrr.2828. https://doi.org/10.1002/dmrr.2828

Stomby, A., Otten, J., Ryberg, M., Andrew, R., Walker, B. R., & Olsson, T. (2020). Diet-induced weight loss alters hepatic glucocorticoid metabolism in type 2 diabetes mellitus. *European Journal of Endocrinology, 182*(4), 447–457. https://doi.org/10.1530/EJE-19-0901

Stomby, A., Otten, J., Ryberg, M., Nyberg, L., Olsson, T., & Boraxbekk, C.-J. (2017). *A Paleolithic Diet with and without Combined Aerobic and Resistance Exercise Increases Functional Brain Responses and Hippocampal Volume in Subjects with Type 2 Diabetes. Frontiers in Aging Neuroscience, 9*. doi:10.3389/fnagi.2017.00391

www.ingramcontent.com/pod-product-compliance
Lightning Source LLC
Chambersburg PA
CBHW081356230426
43667CB00017B/2848